# BIRDS, FLOWERS AND BUTTERFLIES OF THE AMAZON

NORTHWATER

**CONSTANTINE ISSIGHOS**

Copyright 2012 © Constantine Issighos. Published in Canada. Printed in U.S.A. No part of this book may be reproduced or transmitted in any form or by any means, electronic or mechanical, including photocopying, recording, and/or by any information storage and retrieval system except by a reviewer who may quote brief passages in a review to be printed in a magazine, newspaper, or on the web without written permission in writing from the author/publisher. For information, please contact www.awaqkunabooks.com

NorthWater is an imprint of Awaqkuna Books Inc.

**Vol. 12 of THE AMAZON EXPLORATION SERIES:**
*BIRDS, FLOWERS AND BUTTERFLIES OF THE AMAZON*

Library and Archives Canada

ISBN 978-0-9878601-1-8

Library and Archives Canada Cataloguing in Publication

ATTENTION CHILDRENS ASSOCIATIONS, BOOK STORES, PUBLIC OR PRIVATE LIBRARIES: quantity discounts are available on bulk purchases of this book series.

# THE AMAZON EXPLORATION SERIES

Children's Books
by
Constantine Issighos

| | |
|---|---|
| 1 | Upper Amazon Voyage by River Boat |
| 2 | The People of the River |
| 3 | The Children of the River |
| 4 | Amazon's Nature of Things |
| 5 | Echoes of Nature: a Beautiful Wild Habitat |
| 6 | The Amazon Rainforest |
| 7 | Amazonian Sisterhood |
| 8 | Amazon River Wolves |
| 9 | Amazonian Landscapes and Sunsets |
| 10 | Amazonian Canopy: the Roof of the World's Rainforest |
| 11 | Amazonian Tribes: a World of Difference |
| 12 | Birds, Flowers and Butterflies of the Amazon |
| 13 | The Great Wonders of the Amazon |
| 14 | The Jaguar People |
| 15 | The Fresh Water Giants |
| 16 | The Call of the Shaman |
| 17 | Indigenous Families: Life in Harmony with Nature |
| 18 | Amazon in Peril |
| 19 | Giant Tarantulas and Centipedes |
| 20 | The Amazon Ethno-Botanical Garden |
| 21 | The Real Amazon Tribal Warriors |

One of the world's most dazzling spectacles can be found in the Amazon River of South America. If you get up early in the day, you can witness the morning sun clearing the Amazon canopy in the Upper Amazon of Peru, as well as in the south-eastern Manu region. The glaring sun strikes a greyish-pink clay riverbank on the Tambopata River. There, one of the world's most impressive wildlife spectacles is nearing its riotous peak. The steep clay bank has, for thousand of years, been a pulsing 50 meters (150 feet) high palette of red, yellow and green, a veritable winged rainbow.

Thousands upon thousands of parrots squabble over a choice spot to grab a beakful of clay, an important but mysterious part of the parrot's daily diet. Dozens of parrot species visit the clay bank throughout the day. But this morning's commotion belongs to the giant of the parrot world, the macaws.

It is one of the great wonders of the Upper Amazon region— 5,500 kilometres (2.500 miles) north of Manu—in the canopy at 40 meters (120 feet) above the forest floor. At this level thousands of birds of many species argue over choice of mates, nests, and the nutritious seeds and flowers, which form a vital part of their daily diet.

## Macaws

These brightly coloured birds are enormous. Their bodies' measure nearly 1 meter (3 feet) long and they can weight over half a kilo (2 lbs). The macaws belong to the parrot family. Of the 300 different species of parrots throughout the world, almost all of them live in the rainforests. The macaws live in the high trees of the canopies that are located near the riverbanks and coastal areas. They build their nests and lay their eggs at the overstory level–about 30 meters (100 feet) over the canopy level.

With their wide strong wings, macaws can reach speeds of 35 kilometres per hour and they spend most of their day together covering huge distances. At night, macaws roost in large groups to keep them safe from predators, such as monkeys or snakes. They mate for life and are caring parents. Their young ones stay with their parents until they are mature. Macaws share the tropical fruits and nuts they find with their young. Their beaks are well-suited to peel fruits and break nutshells.

The area surrounding the Upper Amazon city of Iquitos is the ultimate bird watching destination in this region. Between January and April, however, it is not always ideal because of the occasional heavy rainstorms.

Walking through the *Allpahuayo-Mishana Reserve* it is as if you are walking through the most perfect of forest paths. The forest on each side is deep green from the ground up. Tiny species of birds have built their nests into every nook and cranny of the tree trunks, and when you look closely you can see the miniature mouths squeaking from within. Every few minutes, brown-winged birds with yellowish bellies fly close by you to drop off a grub. You can also see the magical resplendent *quetzal,* its long green feathers curving down like a quill from its little chubby body.

The *Allpahuayo-Mishana Reserve* is now a famous bird watching site, popularized by the new species of birds that have been found and by a few other enigmatic species. At times, bird watching is slow in the Reserve, but what you see and photograph is typically of very high quality. Though several access sites require permits from officers—a slow process—there are sites where you can pay directly at the entrance. In general the most spectacular bird watching is done near several entrance areas in various types of white sand forests. Night bird watching is a bit difficult because there is no effective protection from mosquitoes.

## Toucans

Of the 42 species of toucans found throughout the world, the majority of them live in the canopies of the rainforests. Toucans are only found in the tropics. The toucan's most recognizable feature is its 7 inch long beak. The beak is hollow and thus surprisingly lightweight. There is as yet no scientific explanation as to why toucans have such an oversized beak. One explanation is that toucans eat small insects, reptiles, fruits and seeds so the large beak helps them eat this variety of foods. The male toucan can grow as large as half a meter (1.5 feet) in length; thus, its beak takes up about half of its body.

Toucans make their nests in small holes inside of hollowed trees. They are very social birds, and they live in pairs and small groups for protection from predators. During the peak of the day's heat, toucans shade themselves in the deep foliage of the canopy.

## Amazonian Parrots

Amazonian Parrots are without a doubt the most beautiful bird species in the entire rainforest. Their popularity is driven by a number of factors, some of which include their rarity in the western world, their beautifully adorned plumage and their ability to talk They can enchant humans by reciting poems, nursery rhymes, songs and words, although not all parrots build up a big vocabulary.

A medium-size parrot measures approximately 35 to 37 cm (6 to7 inches) in length and is predominantly green, yellow or red in colour. The beak is horn and the beak of young parrots is partially grey.

The aggressive nature of Amazonian parrots should never be underestimated. They are famed for their dramatic threatening displays during mating season. If approached, they get excitable and are more likely to attack. They may fly at anyone who intrudes and make lunges in an attempt to scare off anything they perceive as a threat. A good idea would be to leave the parrots alone.

## AMAZON FLORA AND FAUNA

The *Allpahuayo-Mishana Natural Reserve* has been a protected natural environment since 1999. Its total land area is 57,667.43 hectares. This protected ecosystem is very peculiar. A forest of mud and wild flowers on white sand is home to numerous species of flora and fauna, many of which have not been known by scientists. Therefore, the Reserve's function is to protect the Nanay river basin, the white forest, and the more than 1,900 plant species, amongst them almost one hundred whose distribution is very restricted.

Further to the south, in the *Pacay-Samiria Reserve*, scientists have identified more than 1,200 species of flowering plants, grouped into more than a hundred families. Among them are more than 22 species of orchids and 29 species of palm trees. Visitors can find the *aquije* fruit which is appreciated by both humans and animals. It is also quite possible to find a great variety of medicinal flowering plants, the *lupuna* or rubber trees and other big trees that have enormous commercial value.

## Orchids

Most of the Amazon, including the reserves and protected regions, get flooded. The rainy season—usually October to April—is known as "growing," which means that the Amazon River overflows its banks and covers 85% of the protected lands. This ecological situation changes the forest floor turning it into an aquatic field. When the intense rain stops and the river and its tributaries go back to their original beds, hundreds of lagoons and creeks appear thus changing the shape of the landscape from one year to the next. These are the natural conditions under which orchids flourish.

Orchid species make up the largest plant family, occupying almost every diversified habitat. They come in all colours of the rainbow, each with a distinct blossom and environment. Some orchids produce blossoms no larger than a fly, while others have flowers that are larger than a dinner plate.

Although orchids are diverse, each species also has a specific environmental preference. The most particular and picky of the orchid species are only found in certain trees at certain altitudes and only bloom for a few days each year. Other species have different needs depending on where they grow—some grow up only on certain tree-trunks, others require an hour or two of direct sunlight each day, and others need a lot of sun.

## Cat's Claw—Una De Gato

The Amazon rainforest is, in fact, 4 types of forest: the higher areas have the shortest trees and branches; the cloud forest, which is very dense and has a lot of vegetation including ferns and lichens, the mountain forest, and the tropical forest in the lowest lying areas, along the banks of the Amazon river.

The Cat's Claw *(Uncaria tontientosa)* grows in the mountain forest of the Amazon region. It is the most well-known of the medicinal plants. It is a climbing vine that grows in the Andean region between 200 and 800 meters above sea level. Its name, Cat's Claw, comes from the curved thorns located at the lowest level of its stems. The plant is very important due to its medicinal properties which reinforce the immunological system and functions as a natural antibiotic.

Una de gato has been used by many Peruvian tribes, including the "jaguar people," the Ashanikas. It is the Ashanikas who are considered the most knowledgeable about the use of this plant and refer to it as the "Sacred Herb of the Rain Forest." In fact, the Ashanikas have the longest recorded history of experience with this flowering plant, using it to treat the respiratory system, various forms of joint pain and to maintain strong and healthy cardiovascular function.

The Amazon rainforest is a very special place. It is home to many interesting, strange and beautiful birds and flowering plants. Any known number of plants and birds reside in the canopy—the leafy roof of the world's tropical rainforest. Biological interdependency takes many forms in the forest, and pollination and the Amazon's birds and flowers and their role in pollination and seed dispersal are an indispensible part of it.

*The Amazon Exploration Series* *Constantine Issighos*

*Birds, Flowers and Butterflies of the Amazon*

*The Amazon Exploration Series*　　　　　　　　　　*Constantine Issighos*

*Birds, Flowers and Butterflies of the Amazon*

*The Amazon Exploration Series*                                *Constantine Issighos*

*Birds, Flowers and Butterflies of the Amazon*

*The Amazon Exploration Series*                                              *Constantine Issighos*

*The Amazon Exploration Series*            *Constantine Issighos*

*Birds, Flowers and Butterflies of the Amazon*

*The Amazon Exploration Series*                           *Constantine Issighos*

*Birds, Flowers and Butterflies of the Amazon*

www.ingramcontent.com/pod-product-compliance
Lightning Source LLC
Chambersburg PA
CBHW041754040426
42446CB00001B/34